Defining
MOMENTS

Clara
BARTON

I Want to Help!

by Cathy East Dubowski

CONSULTANT
Lynn D. Gordon
Associate Professor of History
University of Rochester

BEARPORT
PUBLISHING COMPANY, INC.

New York, New York

Credits
Cover, Clara Barton National Historic Site; Title page, Clara Barton National
Historic Site; 4, The Granger Collection, New York; 5, Clara Barton National
Historic Site; 6–7 (all), Clara Barton Birthplace Museum; 8, Library of Congress
Prints and Photographs Division Washington, DC; 9, Clara Barton National
Historic Site; 10, Hulton Archive/Getty Images; 11, Clara Barton Birthplace
Museum; 12, Clara Barton National Historic Site; 13, Library of Congress Prints
and Photographs Division Washington, DC; 14, Library of Congress Prints and
Photographs Division Washington, DC; 15 (top), The New York Public Library,
Miriam and Ira D. Wallach Division of Art, Prints and Photographs, (bottom),
The Granger Collection, New York; 16–17 (all), Library of Congress Prints and
Photographs Division Washington, DC; 18, Library of Congress Prints and
Photographs Division Washington, DC; 19, The Granger Collection, New York;
20, AP/Wide World Photos /General Services Administration; 21, Library of
Congress Prints and Photographs Division Washington, DC; 22, Library of
Congress, Washington, DC, Courtesy Clara Barton National Historic Site; 23,
American Red Cross, Hazel Braugh Records Center and Archives Washington,
DC; 24, Clara Barton National Historic Site; 25, Clara Barton Birthplace Museum;
26, Tim Sloan/AFP/Getty Images; 27, American Red Cross, Washington, DC.

Editorial development by Judy Nayer
Design by Fabia Wargin; Production by Luis Leon; Image Research by Jennifer Bright

Library of Congress Cataloging-in-Publication Data
Dubowski, Cathy East.
  Clara Barton : I want to help! / by Cathy East Dubowski.
     p. cm. — (Defining moments)
  Includes bibliographical references and index.
  ISBN 1-59716-075-X (lib. bdg.) — ISBN 1-59716-112-8 (pbk.)
  1. Barton, Clara, 1821–1912—Juvenile literature. 2. American Red Cross—
Biography—Juvenile literature. 3. Nurses—United States—Biography—Juvenile
literature. I. Title. II. Series: Defining moments (New York, N.Y.)

HV569.B3D84 2006
361.7'634'092—dc22

                              2005005223

For more information, write to Bearport Publishing Company, Inc.,
101 Fifth Avenue, Suite 6R, New York, New York 10003.
Printed in the United States of America.

1 2 3 4 5 6 7 8 9 10

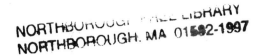

Table of Contents

Courage Under Fire

Clara Barton climbed down from her supply wagon and looked across the cornfield. Cannons boomed in the distance. Bullets whizzed overhead. Black smoke filled the sky.

More than half a million Americans died in the **Civil War**, which lasted from 1861–1865.

The Battle of Antietam (an-TEE-tum) was one of the bloodiest battles of the Civil War.

Clara Barton

Hundreds of soldiers lay on the ground. Clara rushed to help. She brought food, water, and comfort to the soldiers. She helped doctors treat the **wounded**. She even dug a bullet out of a man's cheek with her own pocketknife. When the fighting grew closer, all but one of the male doctors ran away. Clara stayed.

Many people thought Clara was the bravest woman in the world. Few knew that she had grown up scared of everything.

Nothing But Fear

Clara Barton was born on Christmas Day, 1821, in North Oxford, Massachusetts. Her four brothers and sisters were much older than she was. "I had no playmates," she wrote, "but in effect six fathers and mothers." Sometimes they spoiled her. Sometimes they teased her. Other times they forgot all about her.

Stephen Barton

Sarah Stone Barton

Clara's parents

The home where Clara was born is now a museum.

Clara was afraid of almost everything, from thunderstorms to snakes. Most of all, she was afraid of people! She often hid from strangers.

Clara was smart, though. Her brother Stephen taught her math. Her sisters, Dolly and Sally, taught Clara to read by the time she was three years old.

An Eager Nurse

Clara adored her brother David. He taught her to ride horses when she was five years old. He also showed her how to hammer a nail, tie a knot, and throw a ball "like a boy."

When she was nine years old, Clara and her family moved to this house in Massachusetts.

Clara Barton wrote about her childhood in her **autobiography**. It was called *The Story of My Childhood.*

David Barton, as an adult

When Clara was eleven years old, David fell while building a barn. He was badly injured. The doctor was afraid he might die. Clara begged to be her brother's nurse. She learned how to give David his medicine.

Clara never left her brother's side. At last, after nearly two years, David **recovered**. Clara was glad, but she missed being a nurse. She liked the feeling of being needed.

A School to Teach

At seventeen, Clara was still very shy. Her parents worried about her. A family friend believed that the bumps on a person's head could reveal his or her **personality**. He said Clara would never stand up for herself. "But for others she will be perfectly fearless." He suggested that Clara become a teacher.

In the 1800s, children of all ages were often taught together in one-room schoolhouses.

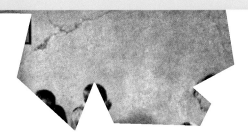

Teachers in Clara's day often spanked or beat children to make them behave. Clara never did.

Clara taught in this schoolhouse in Charlton, Massachusetts.

Clara's parents found her a teaching job. When Clara walked into the classroom, she was too scared to say hello!

Some of the older boys misbehaved. Now Clara's **tomboy** ways came in handy. At recess she joined in the boys' games. They were amazed that she could run and throw a ball so well.

Free Schools for All

Over the years, Clara taught in different schools. Then in 1852, she moved to Bordentown, New Jersey. She was surprised to learn that there were no free schools for the poor.

This is the earliest known photo of Clara. It was taken around 1851, when she was 29 years old.

Clara decided to start a school and to teach for free. On the first day, only six boys showed up. Clara taught as if the room were full. The next day 20 children came. Soon she had more than 600 students.

The townspeople were delighted. They voted to build a new school. When the school opened, though, they chose a man to be the principal. Clara was crushed. So, she **resigned**.

Clara's school in Bordentown was the first free school in New Jersey.

War Breaks Out

In 1854, Clara moved to Washington, D.C.
She got a job in the U.S. **Patent** Office as a **clerk**.
In a time when most women married and raised
a family, Clara earned as much as a man.

The U.S. Patent Office, where Clara worked as a clerk

Meanwhile, the issue of slavery was tearing the country apart. Many people in the Northern states wanted to end slavery. Many in the South believed that each state should decide about slavery for itself. The two sides argued bitterly. They could not reach an agreement. On April 12, 1861, Southern **rebels** fired on Fort Sumter in South Carolina. The Civil War had begun.

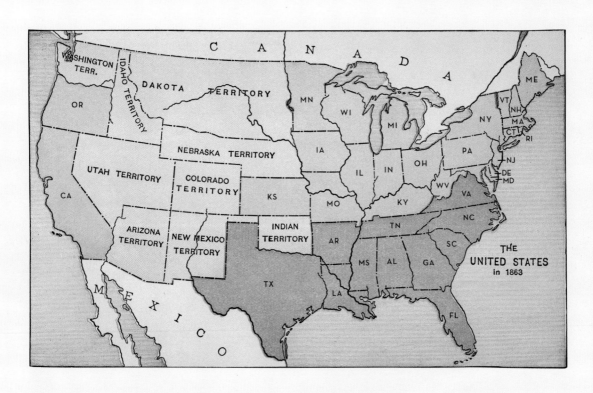

The green-colored states fought to keep slavery legal.

Clara Finds a New Cause

Thousands of army **volunteers** headed to Washington, D.C. When Clara learned that many were her old students, she rushed to help. She brought them food and other **necessities**. She wrote letters to friends and relatives and put ads in newspapers, asking for supplies. Soon, packages came pouring in.

Soldiers training at a camp just outside Washington, D.C.

Soldiers who fought for the North made up the Union Army. Soldiers who fought for the South were part of the Confederate Army.

A Union soldier

A Confederate soldier

Many thought the war would be over in a few months. Instead it lasted four long years.

At first Clara helped wounded soldiers returning from battle. She was shocked by their news. Food and medicine took days to reach the armies. Soldiers were dying because there were not enough doctors, nurses, and supplies to save them.

Angel of the Battlefield

Clara wanted to go where she was most needed—the battlefield. For a long time the War Department said that women did not belong there. Finally, in July 1862, Clara got permission to take supplies to a battlefield near Culpeper, Virginia. When she arrived, the doctors were out of bandages. Clara saved the day.

Culpeper, Virginia

Clara helps a wounded soldier on the battlefield.

Clara served on battlefields in Virginia, South Carolina, and Georgia. She braved gunfire and went without food. She delivered supplies, cooked meals, nursed wounds, and wrote down the final words of dying soldiers. One doctor called her the "angel of the battlefield."

A Search for the Missing

After the war ended on April 9, 1865, Clara returned to Washington, D.C. There, she found a new cause. More than half a million soldiers had died. Many more were injured. Thousands were missing. Clara helped friends and relatives find out what happened to their loved ones.

In an age with no phones, TVs, or Internet, Clara became a **clearinghouse** for information. Newspapers even printed a letter from President Lincoln to "the Friends of Missing Persons." He told people to write to Clara with information.

The sign from Clara's office

Clara received thousands of letters. People wrote to her with names or news. She found information on more than 22,000 soldiers.

Clara and a soldier named Dorence Atwater helped uncover information about thousands of soldiers who died at Andersonville Prison in Georgia.

Clara was chosen to raise the flag at the dedication of Andersonville Cemetery on August 17, 1865.

A New Way to Serve

A few years later, Clara went to Geneva, Switzerland. There she met Dr. Louis Appia. He told her about an **organization** called the **International** Red Cross. The group delivered food, clothing, and medical care to people in times of war. Thirty-two nations had already joined the Red Cross.

Clara was the first American woman to receive Germany's highest honor, the Iron Cross, for her work during the Franco-Prussian war.

Clara with dozens of Red Cross nurses

In 1870, war broke out in Europe. Clara stayed as a volunteer for the Red Cross. She gave out supplies to families that needed help.

In 1873, Clara returned home with the Red Cross as her new cause. In 1881, she succeeded in creating the American Red Cross. At age 59, she became its first president.

The American Red Cross

Clara thought that the Red Cross could do more than help in times of war. She believed it should also be ready during peacetime to help people hurt by natural **disasters**, such as fires and floods.

In 1889, Clara brought help and hope to victims of a flood in Johnstown, Pennsylvania.

Clara was in her seventies when she took her Red Cross work to Cuba during the Spanish-American War.

The International Red Cross was so impressed by Clara's work that they changed their **treaty** to include disaster relief. They called it the American Amendment.

In 1882, Clara rented a steamboat to take supplies to people in Ohio and Indiana. Their lives had been destroyed by floods. In 1893, she brought food and clothing to people in the Sea Islands, off the coast of South Carolina. A hurricane had left them homeless. As always, Clara was the first to arrive and the last to leave.

Her Work Lives On

At age 83, Clara resigned after 23 years as president of the American Red Cross. Still, she stayed busy. She started the First Aid Society to teach people about basic first aid. She also wrote books about her life.

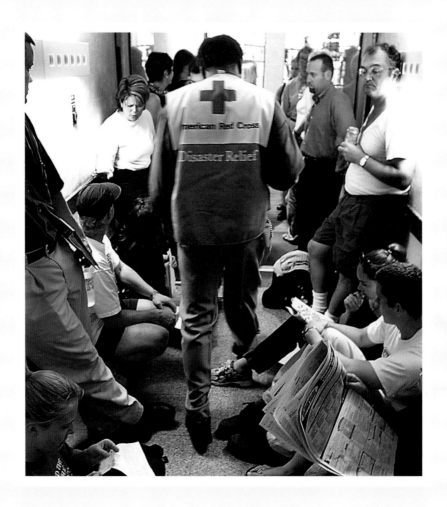

Red Cross workers ran a blood drive following the terrorist attacks on September 11, 2001.

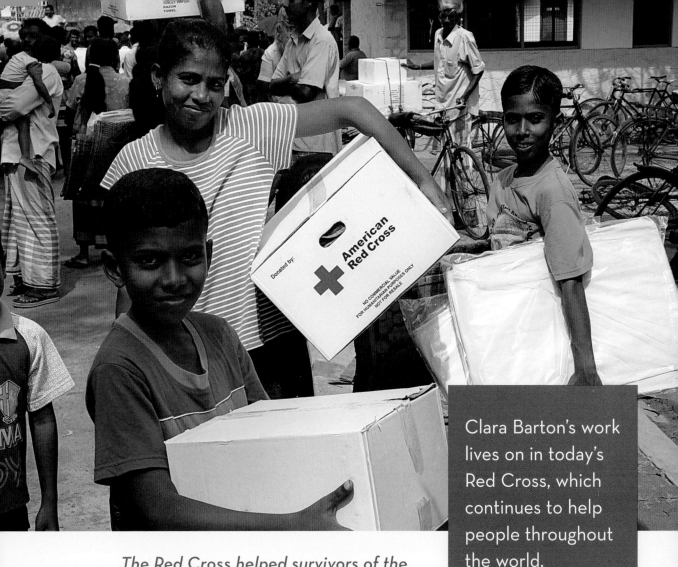

Clara Barton's work lives on in today's Red Cross, which continues to help people throughout the world.

The Red Cross helped survivors of the 2004 tsunami in the Indian Ocean.

On April 12, 1912, Clara died at her home in Glen Echo, Maryland. She was 90 years old.

Timid and shy as a child, Clara Barton faced cannon fire and floods to bring comfort and hope to thousands. In an age when most women married and stayed at home, she bravely carved out her own path and devoted her life to helping others.

Just the Facts

■ Clara Barton's full name was Clarissa Howe Barton. However, everyone called her Clara.

■ When Clara was five years old, her brothers taught her to ride a horse. This skill came in handy much later, when Clara had to leave the battlefield in a hurry during the Civil War.

Timeline

Here are some important events in the life of Clara Barton.

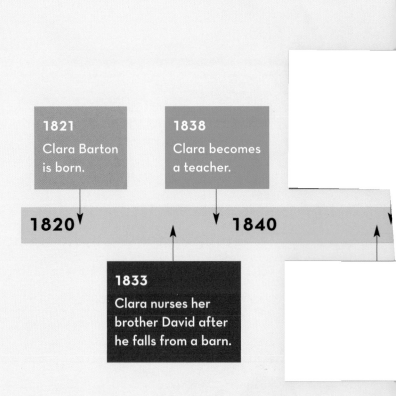

1821
Clara Barton is born.

1838
Clara becomes a teacher.

1820

1840

1833
Clara nurses her brother David after he falls from a barn.

Once, on the battlefield, Clara leaned down to give a wounded soldier some water. A bullet flew between them! It tore a hole in her sleeve and killed the man. Clara bravely kept working.

■ After the Civil War, Clara gave talks to raise money for her work finding lost soldiers. Giving speeches was not easy for someone so shy.

■ Clara loved cats. A senator once sent Clara a kitten to thank her for her work at the Battle of Antietam.

■ Clara was the first woman ever to serve as an ambassador for the United States government.

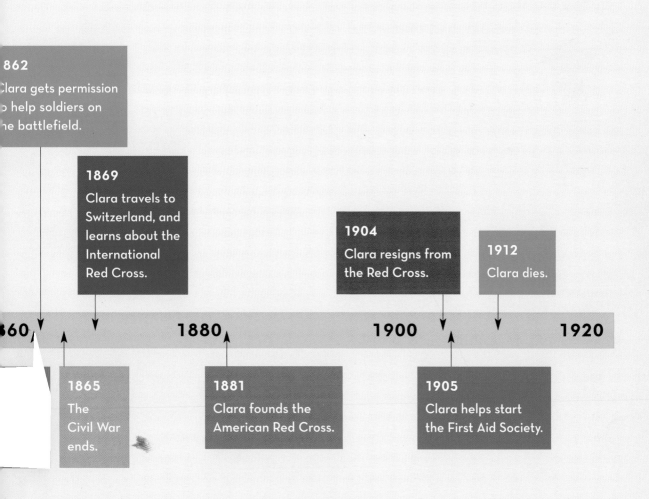

1862
Clara gets permission to help soldiers on the battlefield.

1869
Clara travels to Switzerland, and learns about the International Red Cross.

1904
Clara resigns from the Red Cross.

1912
Clara dies.

1860   **1880**   **1900**   **1920**

1865
The Civil War ends.

1881
Clara founds the American Red Cross.

1905
Clara helps start the First Aid Society.

Glossary

autobiography (*aw*-toh-bye-OG-ruh-fee) a book in which the author tells the story of his or her life

Civil War (SIV-il WOR) the U.S. war between the Southern states and the Northern states, that lasted from 1861–1865

clearinghouse (KLIHR-ing-*houss*) a place (or person) that collects and sends out information

clerk (KLURK) a person who keeps records in an office

disasters (duh-ZASS-turz) terrible acts of nature that happen suddenly and cause much damage

international (*in*-tur-NASH-uh-nuhl) involving two or more countries

necessities (nuh-SESS-uh-tees) basic things that are needed in order to live, such as food, clothing, and shelter

organization (*or*-guh-nuh-ZAY-shuhn) a group of people with a common interest or purpose

patent (PAT-uhnt) a document giving an inventor the right to make, use, and sell his or her invention

personality (*pur*-suh-NAL-uh-tee) all the character traits that make a person who he or she is

rebels (REB-uhlz) people who fight against those in charge; the Confederate soldiers were called rebels

recovered (ri-KUHV-urd) got better or well after an illness

resigned (ri-ZINED) gave up, or quit, a job

tomboy (TOM-*boi*) a girl who likes to do things once thought of as activities just for boys

treaty (TREE-tee) an agreement between two or more countries

volunteers (*vol*-uhn-TIHRZ) people who offer to do a job without being paid

wounded (WOON-did) people who are hurt during a war

Bibliography

Barton, Clara. *The Story of My Childhood.* New York: Arno Press (1980).

Dubowski, Cathy East. *Clara Barton: Healing the Wounds.* Englewood Cliffs, NJ: Silver Burdett Press (1991).

Oates, Stephen B. *A Woman of Valor: Clara Barton and the Civil War.* New York: The Free Press (1994).

Pryor, Elizabeth Brown. *Clara Barton, Professional Angel.* Philadelphia, PA: University of Pennsylvania Press (1987).

Read More

Lakin, Patricia. *Clara Barton: Spirit of the American Red Cross.* New York: Aladdin Paperbacks (2004).

Mara, Wil. *Clara Barton.* Danbury, CT: Children's Press (2002).

Ransom, Candice. *Clara Barton.* New York: Barnes & Noble Books (2003).

Raum, Elizabeth. *Clara Barton.* Chicago, IL: Heinemann Library (2004).

Learn More Online

Visit these Web sites to learn more about Clara Barton and the Red Cross:

www.clarabartonbirthplace.org
www.nps.gov/clba/
www.redcross.org

Index

About the Author

CATHY EAST DUBOWSKI has written many books for children and adults. She lives in Chapel Hill, North Carolina.